The Pharaocracy of America and Niihau

From Iniki to Empire

Horus Michael

The Pharaocracy of America and Niihau

From Iniki to Empire

This book was printed in the U.S.A.

www.amazon.com/author/horusmichael

Genre: Political Science

(6x9 B&W)

(*This book is a product of the UEIR*)

The Pharaocracy of America and Niihau

From Iniki to Empire

Preface:

In case the USA Government shuts down, for whatever reason: economical, debt foreclosure, rebellion, Budget impasse, or politics, know that there will be a Government in place afterwards (not the Shadow Government) – that being, THIS ONE. So until that fateful day passes, this book is an optional replacement to the United States' Constitution.

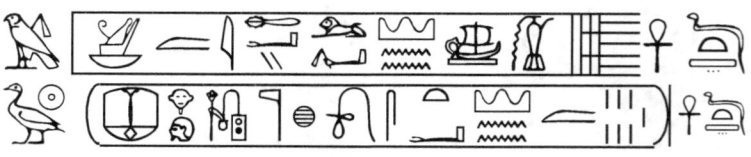

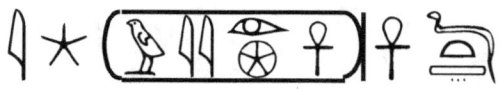

Chapter 1: Statistics

In the **Summer of 1992** the American-Russian Cold War finally ended with the Conquest of the USA Federal Government by Lord S7, and the Conquest of the USSR the previous year. This Summer had a glimpse of *Elemental Chronokinetic Energy* (or as they say in religion, the "Power of God") resulting in 2 mentally-influenced Hurricanes, one (**Andrew**) in Florida, the other (**Iniki**) **in Hawaii**. These cataclysms were the equivalent of dropping 2 Atomic Bombs onto Japan in World War 2, forcing their surrender. The American President was warned of his behavior, post-Iraq war of 1991, when he went about trashing every "dictator and tyrant" on television, and for insulting a *Netherworld Sultan* with the motto ascribed to the Democratic Political Party, calling them "*those Sultans of Status Quo.*" Lord S7 was reincarnated American President **Jack Kennedy**, who desired to return in a new body and "conquer Russia and USA" to end the Cold War; this data was a closely-guarded **secret** of the CIA, whom later classified Lord S7 "top secret" due to "Divine origin." Elemental ability is not studied in schools as it is rare – unless you think like Moses of the Israelites. The USA surrendered to "the Supreme, Eternal...Sovereign Lord (God)" on January 20, 1993 before Bill Clinton was sworn in as President, *before* saying "So help me, ... God." This is because "Gods cause weather anomalies" traditionally, and due to the use of titles by S7.

Elementals are **not** story book characters. They are placed **in** stories by imaginative people, and exist **outside of** stories as **Elemental Psychics**. People with this rare ability have always existed, less so in the Ancient World, more so today with multiples in population. Genetics has a key in this. People from Occult backgrounds have it. People whose families were sorcerers, priests, magicians, wizards, etc., have the **gene** for this ability. Not all of them are famous. Some drew pictures in *Neanderthal caves* which influenced their hunting families. Others wrote books that influenced Time after being read (Michael Nostradame). Some became saviors like Joan of Arc or Christ, later *sacrificed* by an ignorant or envious population. Not all made religions out of their talent. But for those who have it, they will know how to save society from itself, by writing books like this one with their ability in focus.

The American President, **George Herbert** Walker Bush, **was identified with** Tutankhamon's *nemesis*, **George Herbert** Stanhope M. Carnarvon, the English royal who funded the excavation of KV62 and desired the golden burial for his Castle. For unclear reasons, Lord S7 decided to become angry with the President while vacationing in Louisiana; the location was bad from a *Reincarnation* standpoint – never stay long in an area of one's past. Napoleon Bonaparte sold Louisiana to USA, and he also started Egyptology and the tomb excavations leading up to KV62 (Tutankhamon) in 1922. The Kennedy White House had "French Empire décor" so that was bad too. So Lord S7 as JFK wanted to conquer the world with his future Elemental powers, as studied by the CIA during the Cold War (i.e. *Psychic Warfare*). This was remembered while in New Orleans, prior to attracting Hurricane Andrew en route to the West, and Iniki to Hawaii. **Tutankhamon always had a temper problem...**

Meanwhile in California, a book circulated that put a mythology to Lord S7. This book was *Eye of the Pharaoh* ©1990, 1995. The character **modeled after** Lord S7 was **identified with** S7 to clarify that people were reading it (*it was stolen by a reviewer and published in 1992 as a true-story*). The book

was fiction, until it started to influence Destiny (Time) once read by people. It is not completely fictional now, so the US Government *classified it top secret and confiscated the stolen proceeds, never paying its top-secret author.* **Rumors said** the proceeds exceed $900 Billion USD by 2007 CE, from Black Market sales. All data after 1994 is conjecture.

Lord S7 went on a global conquest spree that resulted in global Climate Change or Global Warming using Elemental ability. Earthquakes and Tsunamis are **not caused** by CC. Indonesia claimed to have started an army to "combat **the Antichrist**" in 1997 or 1999. In 2004 it was hit by a Tsunami the day *after* Christmas, and in 2005 by an Earthquake the day *after* Easter; both are Christian holidays. People who read the book believed the character (or author) was this entity. In the Bible, Christ causes Earthquakes and influences Storms. Antichrist is **not** supposed to be divine or supernatural; he (she) uses human technology. Anyway, Indonesia was conquered.

For reasons in the process of conquest, Lord S7 created Government codes for his Divine Empire; you know, in case people shrugged off civilization every time they are conquered. This may be a waste of time, but educative.

Lord S7 (speaking in Julius Caesar's 3rd person) told Pres. Bush to go to Iraq in 1991, in fears of the **Iraqi Empire seizing the OPEC oil fields** in the East after they invaded Kuwait. So USA did, and they had help in the region. When Bush's son came to power, he used the 9-11-2001 excuse to invade Iraq and "finish the job of his father." September 11, 1992 was two-fold: one it was the same day Hurricane Iniki hit Hawaii; and two, it was New Year's Day in Coptic Christianity (Egyptian Christians). September 11, 2001 was the day **(we are told)** that an Islamic terrorist group (Al Qaeda) attacked the USA using airplanes in **Kamikaze** formation (the Kamikaze idea was in the 1996 UEIR Plebeian Law Code). **This sounds fake, scripted.** Why sacrifice people as an excuse to overthrow Iraq? Use peoples' emotions against an enemy that did not exist until CIA created them. Pres. Bush Sr. was formerly a Director of the CIA – which is how he made his son President, via connections in Government.

Unless you want to kiss Saddam's ring for $100 a gallon of gasoline, the invasion was necessary. Now we have an Islamic Caliphate occupying Iraq (2014). Was this a fair trade? The 2011 Arab Spring – or "Democracy in the Middle East" – was written in that **book** along with "wars" against the Arab-Terrorist States, which wrote the "war on terrorism" of Pres. George W. Bush after 2001. The book was written from July 1988 to March 1990 ©MC. **Everything happens in 10 year intervals:**

1981 – Egypt's President Anwar al-Sadat was assassinated.

1991 – Iraq invasion of Kuwait, Operation Desert Shield & Storm.

2001 – Al Qaeda "attacks USA."

2011 – The Arab Spring, Democracy Movement overthrows Egypt & Tunisia.

Post-Conquest **protocol** in USA involved **busywork** – they "advertised the UEIR" in mass media for "communication purposes." This ranged from commercials, product names or symbols, hotel designs, films, content in films as relating to the UEIR propaganda, costumes, colors, handlebar moustaches, ionic pillars, yin-yang (wing-dings language code), SNL, etc. This started in 1993 and continues past 2014.

Hey, it's either that, or they build me a **Pyramid** or some monument.

So Lord S7 is stuck with a book that **no one** but a dead Egyptian Queen was supposed to read that is slowly becoming real, and a large population of people subscribing to gossip mills. Nonetheless, the work continues (*until the author of said book is paid or compensated*).

In 1992 the **Island of Niihau** was **hit by Iniki. It was hit very hard.** In July 2000 M7 asked the US Government to purchase it for $2B USD (with *Eye of the Pharaoh* proceeds **they said** they were keeping for him). On Wikipedia.com an entry in 2014 said the "Federal Government offered over $1 Billion USD to buy the island" **but** "was refused." In 2002 the island's (former) owner died, leaving her heirs with **excuses** relating to how she kept this knowledge from them. One of them decided to **create an ecosystem** on the island, **to prevent development**. If they don't accept the island's legal purchase, will they accept its Conquest in 1992? Hawaii was united by the Conquests of King Kamehameha. Niihau was not conquered by him, rather, it was purchased. After 2000 M7 decided to "make a country out of Niihau" using "Micronation ideas." This project exists on websites and in books by M7.

After 2004 M7 had an issue with some unscrupulous **neighbors** who were mentioned in *Eye of the Pharaoh, chapter 18.* They started an illegal **investigation** into M7's classified top secret & personal data and the real estate he wanted the US Gov to purchase on his behalf (for Nation building). Some of them threatened a lawsuit to extort his billions, or claim Niihau as theirs. They were **arrested** once the FBI was contacted.

Niihau and the classified intelligence **were made public**. M7 had to create counter intelligence to stop the interest of the public in his personal life or classified one. The neighbors are still collecting data, mostly for gossip in the false belief that M7 "was famous." On Sept. 12, 2001 one of them was on his cellular phone and asked to speak directly to *Osama bin Laden of Al Qaeda.* "Do you know our neighbor? M7 & all that? Can you do to him what you did to the USA?" This call was traced by UEIR and rerouted telepathically. M7 has a telepathic frequency [**Telepsi**] that **interferes with cell phone or radio broadcasts**. M7 used this frequency to purchase Niihau on July 5, 2000 after 11:30pm. The following day an art dealer in

Kauai asked M7 if he was "going to buy him out" of his artwork; rumors spread fast in Hawaii. **Niihau** is the ***Forbidden Island*** where Native Hawaiians live on a sort of Hawaiian Reservation land, closed to **all** outsiders. M7 is a **Hawaiian Akua** (divine person); so he called his island nation, "Akua Niihau." M7 had ancestors who were plantation owners in Hawaii. M7's magical power, or **Mana**, is rich in Hawaii. Whenever he visits Hawaii the Mana is noticeable, especially with Games of Chance.

Statistics:

Government type: Pharaocracy

National Anthem: Conch Shell (1.5 Minutes exhale)

National Religion: Pharaohism

Ruler: Pharaoh (1), Council of Viziers (51; includes 50 USA States plus 1 for Niihau; One Vizier per State; non-State Provinces have Consuls). The Vizierate is a Senate of Viziers.

Laws: Code Maat (Code Caesar series).

National Animal: Blue Whale (or Monk Seal)

National Flower: White Lotus flower.

National Beverage: Arnold Palmer (½ Iced tea, ½ Lemonade)

National Pastime: Computer Games

Motto: *"When Science fails, Fantasy prevails."*

National Currency: Kahelelani (Kah.); 1 Kah= $1000 USD. Currency is finite, and can be traded or cashed in for shells when available.

Taxes: **10% or Tithe** of Population per 2 Month Interval; unless exempted (Ex: disabled, elderly, Pharaoh, Veteran, etc.). **No Sales Taxes or other Taxes.**

Debts: If debts are **not paid** in 3 Years' Time the debt is voided by Law and the Credit Rating is lowered by 0.01% each time as incentive to pay debts on time (This is called *The Debt-Tender Law*).

Military Budget: In USA if you give the Military $100 Billion USD, what do they spend this on? They buy 4 $25B each worth of a State-of-the-Art (SOTA) Fighter Jet or Tank/weapon. With $100B you can purchase 400,000 Soldier supplies for one year at low cost, generic non-brand name prices. So don't waste money on SOTA items, then ask for more when the fund dries up or with Credit spending. **Buy low cost items**; they are more plentiful when funding is not wasted; **Needs come *before* Wants.**

Technology: ideas come from USA and are stolen elsewhere. **Focus** more **on training** than technology, less research to steal. Less trained soldiers with Technology = equals higher casualties (dead soldiers) in war.

Alternative Punishments over Prisons: Prisons waste funds; do not solve problems, occupy space, and prisoners retain the same feelings or ideas until released, or are educated in crime while there. Examples of alternatives include: Public Humiliation (wear sign in public with crimes listed for one month), College Fraternity Hazing, Flogging with whip, Subliminal counter programming (television with psychedelic drugs), Forced Poverty (similar to stripped of rights, but without money for 1 year), Shock or Water-boarding, Peace Corps or island exile.

Military Conscription: Psychic Warfare soldiers are recruited once they are proven to have an ability worth exploiting; age 17+ to 55 years of age. They need **not** be sent to a foreign country and can work in PAN.

Psychic Warfare Soldiers should read the book, *"Effective Egyptian Magic Spells © Horus Michael, 2014"* or its equivalent.

Normal Soldiers in USA must be trained in **both** tactical and *imaginative* combat. **Imaginative** means use **your intellect** to solve problems or situations, and explore ideas mentally before attacking an enemy. **American Soldiers must complete 2 years of Junior College first before deployment**, and should **not** be married, engaged, have children, or other means of ***exploitation*** by the enemy. There must be **no distractions** if we are to win the wars against the terrorists or religious cult extremists (AQ). Distractions are like using a cell phone while driving; or not paying attention to what you are doing and then cause something bad accidentally. They **must also** be **trained in** First Aid, 2+ Martial Arts (defense and offense), Meditation (to prevent PTSD), weapons technology, the Enemy whom they are to combat, **with college courses in** Military History (from Thutmose 3 to General Colin Powell), Emergency Infrastructure, Communications, Engineering, Mathematics, Physical Science, Computer Science, Napoleon's Maxims, **or** City Planning.

Military Veterans form the **Imperial Guard**, a form of Post-Military/Police Force, which enforces the laws of the nation. This assures an occupation after Military work concludes. Otherwise the Police force is a Government-regulated, **private company or corporation** – as American Ambulance Companies are **separate from** any government. So Firemen, Police, Hospitals, Technologies, Postal workers, etc. **are all private companies owned by the Pharaocracy of America and Ni'ihau**. This is better than using **taxes** to pay for their services, in an effort to **repay American debt** for the *next thousand years*.

PAN taxes pay for the Pharaocracy (Pharaoh & his Court, Palaces, general maintenance, insignia, servants, Temples & Priesthood, etc.), the Viziers (law makers and enforcers), the Imperial Treasury (savings, & bank), real estate owned by Pharaoh, and the Imperial Guard; **all other taxes at present are to repay the American Debts incurred** from mismanagement of State Funding or credit purchases by previous corrupt rulers. Once that is complete, the funds go to a General Fund Pool or the Imperial Treasury and other Temple "Granaries." **Taxes** will also go to the **author of** *Eye of the Pharaoh* ©1990 **if not paid by** the proceeds of said classified book.

Tax Exemptions:

Pharaoh & His Court (The Pharaocracy), Viziers, the Vizierate, Viceroys of the Military (our word for General of the Army or representative of the Military), Temples & Priests, Akua / Neteru incarnate or visible, Veterans of the Military or Foreign Dignitaries, Disabled people, the Elderly, people with fixed incomes or listed as Poor (below 30 Kah per year, or $30,000 USD), non-residents, homeless people, criminals in prison, children, pets, Natives of Niihau, and the like **are Exempt from Taxes.**

Taxes may be paid by: Bank Check, Niihau Shells, Kahelelani Currency, Barter, Precious Metals or Stones, Paycheck deductions, Real Estate acquisitions, Company Products (from Companies), Services Credit, unopened packaged Food & Drink/Clothing/ textiles, labor, Time Credits (Time Dollars); favors, cooperation, good will, obedience, etc.

Physical Tax revenue may be paid by Bank Check, Cash, Precious Metals/Stones, Service Credits, book royalties, or IRS Refunds.

Taxes are to be collected or sent bi-monthly or **at least twice per year** (Solstices).

Chapter 2: Code of Maat

(Code Caesar Series)

Introduction:

The **Code Caesar** is the Official Provincial Civil Code for the UEIR on Earth. It is named after *Gaius Julius Caesar*, the original designer or **Founder of the UEIR** (and would have been official if the *Ides of March* event never happened).

Each Province constitutes an annexed land or conquered vassal of the UEIR, and is governed by a Consul or King. One must be at least some form of King or its equivalent to serve as a Senator in the Imperial Senate. This is the *Kingdom of God* in the Osirian (later, Christian) prophecy.

UEIR Laws are enforced by **Angels** and other spiritual beings. Each Citizen is assigned a Guardian Angel (**Akhu**) to protect and guide him or her. These are summonable from Duat. UEIR Laws are also enforced by Psychic Commands or "Magic" / "Heka." Kheri-Heb Priests, Kahuna Priests, etc. can give orders to Angels for enforcement.

Punishment for violations can exist on Earth or in Duat; negative events are common (fires, accidents, Natural Disasters/Acts of God, floods, quakes, tsunamis, economic factors/recessions, etc.). A permanent punishment can take the form of a curse or jinx, until dispelled by an Official of Government (UEIR). Each level is numerical, and begins with one level, and can escalate due to severity of crime.

Crimes and Levels of Punishment:

1. **Warning.** Given as a Citation for an accident, infraction, disturbance of Peace, or premeditation of a crime without action.
2. **Minor.** Low level Crime that incurs a Fine; can be paid with money, barter exchange, labor, Time Credits, Community Service, other compensation, and multiplies in amount by 10% in coin per count of future crimes.
3. **Major.** High level Crime that incurs a Heavy Fine, unpaid labor (construction of monuments, buildings, or mental layout if physical disability is present), Community Service (one month per crime), Deprogramming Sessions in a Mental Facility (for violent crimes or multiple theft crimes), medication, branding with Bar Code for Tracking Purposes (if imprisoned by foreign nation or released), Limited Removal of Citizen (or Plebe) Rights, etc.
4. **Permanent.** Top Level Crime that incurs 150% of a Heavy Fine, Natural Disaster, exile, Divine Execution and transference to Duat for Judgment, banishment, the equivalent of Life in Prison (USA), and removal of Citizen Rights for duration decided by Courts; or physical / mental punishment(s).

List of Violations with Number of level:

STEALING:

Armed robbery: 3

Normal, unarmed robbery: 2

Theft of items: 2

Theft of Valuables: 2, 3

Theft of Food in a Store: 1, 2

Shoplifting: 2

Major Shoplifting: 3

Copyright Infringement: 2, 3

Plagiarism (unpaid, Cultural): 2

Plagiarism (paid): 2, 3

Mugging (on a public street): 2, 3

Kidnapping (people): 3

Kidnapping (animal): 2, 3

Computer or Internet theft: 2

File Sharing (paid): 2

In Computer Game (online): 1, 2

Embezzlement (paid): 3

Conspiracy to Steal: 2, 3

Patent Theft: 2, 3

Piracy, (real or online): 2, 3

Computer Hacking: 2, 3

STEALING:

Stealing Personal Data: 2, 3

Data Mining or Phishing: 2, 3

Crookedness: 2, 3

Price Gouging, Petty Theft: 2, 3

Market Manipulation: 2, 3

Deceptive Advertising: 2, 3

Deceiving Elderly or Disabled: 3

Obtaining Classified Data: 3

Other Computer Theft: 2, 3

Computer Viruses (use): 3

Key loggers: 3

Key Duplication (non-owner): 2, 3

Cloning (non-medical): 2, 3

Conquering (non-UEIR): 3

From Temples, Churches: 2, 3

From (Education) Facilities: 2, 3

From States: 2, 3

From Pharaoh: 3

False Advertising: 2, 3

Mail Fraud: 2, 3

False Business: 2, 3

Con Artistry (paid): 3

Entrapment: 3

STEALING:

Eavesdropping (non-personal): 2

Wire-Tapping (Personal): 2, 3

Espionage (non-UEIR): 3

Agricultural Theft: 2, 3

Artifact Theft: 3

Hoarding (paid): 2, 3

Photocopying (non-personal): 1, 2

Forgery of Currency: 3

Forgery of Artifacts: 3

Forgery of UEIR Government: 3

False Claims: 2, 3

False Inheritance Claims: 2, 3

False Charity: 2, 3

Unofficial Marketing: 2, 3

Grand Theft: 2, 3

Hidden Fees: 2, 3

Immoral Company TOS: 3

Waiving Personal Rights: 2, 3

Undisclosed Fees: 2, 3

Lead Coins (not gold): 2, 3

Other Stealing: 2, 3

KILLING:

Abortion (multiple, Late Term): 2, 3

Abortion (inconvenience): 2, 3

Abortion (non-genetic defect): 2, 3

Premeditated, multiple (Serial Killing): 3

Mass Murder, Genocide: 3, 4

Murder-Suicide: 3, 4

Attempted Murder-Suicide: 3

Terrorism with Murder: 3, 4

Terrorism with Malice: 3

Terrorism with Destruction: 3

Assault with Weapons: 2, 3

Assault with Intent to Kill: 3

Unintentional Assault: 2, 3

Accidental Assault with Weapon: 1, 2

Accidental Assault: 1, 2

Accidental Killing (person): 2

Accidental Killing (other): 2

Driving with Intent: 3

Driving Accidental Death: 2

Driving with Distraction: 2, 3

DUI (alcohol or drugs): 2, 3

DUI with Internet: 2, 3

DUI (multiple): 3

KILLING:

Cannibalism (human): 3

Sports Killing (Endangered Species): 2, 3

Hunting (non-Food; non-Niihau): 2

Technology Abuse (animals): 2, 3

Chemical use (on people): 2, 3

Killing with Big Weapons (WMD): 3

Nuclear War: 3, 4

Deity Impersonation: 2, 3

Rioting: 2, 3

Military Incursion: 3

Protesting (armed): 3

Protesting (peaceful): 1, 2

Subversion: 3

Peaceful Terrorism: 2

Anarchy, Supporting Hostility: 3

Religious Terrorism: 2

Destruction of Property: 2, 3

Vandalism, Effacement: 2, 3

Destroying Monuments: 3, 4

Extremism with Violence: 3

Paid Assassination: 3, 4

Assassination: 3, 4

Conspiracy to Kill: 3

KILLING:

Attempting to overthrow Government: 3

Killing Ecosystem: 2, 3

Medical Testing Abuse (animals): 2, 3

Food Procurement Abuse (animals): 3

Animal Abuse: 2, 3

Human Abuse: 2, 3

Other Abuse: 2, 3

Elderly Abuse & Neglect: 2, 3

Assisted Suicide: 2, 3

Attempted Suicide or Murder: 2, 3

Suicide (as a Weapon): 3, 4

Forced Suicide: 3

Drug use that kills: 2, 3

Medical Malpractice: 3

Dental Malpractice: 2, 3

Single Murder: 3

Manslaughter (unintended Killing): 2, 3

Internet Hoax that results in Death: 3

Killing Police or Government (UEIR): 3

Assaulting Police or Government (UEIR): 2, 3

Poisoning: 2, 3

Causing Diseases: 2, 3

Other Killing: 2, 3

DECEPTION:

Lying under Oath: 2, 3

Lying to God(s): 3

Lying to Goddess(es): 3

Lying to Angels: 2, 3

Deceptive Behavior: 2

Forged Documents: 2, 3

Forgeries in General: 2, 3

Deception of TOS: 3

Un-disclosure of Facts: 2, 3

Deceptive Marketing: 2, 3

Deceptive Documentation: 2, 3

Industrial Espionage: 3

Lying in Court: 2, 3

Political Deception: 3

Contract Deception: 2, 3

Terms of Service Deception: 2, 3

Stealing Passwords, Impersonation: 3

Identity Theft: 3

Overall Crookedness: 3

Corruption (bribery, extortion): 2, 3

General Conspiracy: 3

Greed; Envy, Wrath, Sloth, Lust, etc.: 2, 3

Deliberate "Stupidity": 1, 2

DECEPTION:

Bringing False Witness(es): 3

False Pedigree, Education: 2, 3

False Rank (Military, Police): 2, 3

Dressing as Government (UEIR): 2, 3

Using Same Insignia as UEIR (M7): 3

False Pretending: 2

False Imprisonment (by Foreign Police, etc.): 2

False Valor (UEIR): 2

False Inheritance: 2, 3

Political Incorrectness: 2

Forgery of (Niihau) Shells: 3

Forgery of Precious Metals, items: 3

Copyright Deception: 3

Patent Deception: 2, 3

Immoral Gossip: 2, 3

Slander or Libel: 3

Malicious Rumors: 3

Making People Cry from Deception: 2

Deceptive Terrorism: 2, 3

Disrespect (of Citizens, UEIR): 2

Deceptive Quality of Products: 2, 3

Other Deception: 2, 3

DESTRUCTION:

Assault, multiple: 2, 3

Assault, single: 2

Assault, mental: 2

Assault, minor (slap): 2

Assault with Weapon: 2, 3

Assault with training: 2, 3

Assault, military: 3

General Violence: 2

Vandalism, Graffiti: 2, 3

Monument Destruction: 3

Religious element: 2, 3

Religious Extremist: 2, 3

Terrorism, destruction: 3

Explosives (non-military): 2, 3

Illegal Fireworks: 2, 3

IED Device: 3

Booby-trap: 2, 3

Snare, Trip Wire: 2, 3

Grenade (non-UEIR): 2, 3

Bombs on Vehicle: 3

Laser Weapons, (Non-UEIR): 3

Chemical, Nuclear Weapons: 3

Biological Weapons: 3

DESTRUCTION:

Psychic Weapons (Non-UEIR): 3

Psychic War (Non-UEIR): 3, 4

General War (non-UEIR): 3

War Crimes (non-UEIR): 3, 4

Crimes against God(s): 3, 4

Crimes against Earth: 3

Crimes against Humanity (Chaos): 2, 3

Crimes against Nature: 3

Vehicle Destruction: 2, 3

Private Property Damage: 2, 3

Sign Post Damage: 2

Infrastructure Damage: 2

Poisoning Water System: 3

Exploding a Device: 3

Airplane bombings: 3, 4

Transportation Terrorism: 3, 4

Animal Provocation, bites: 2, 3

Torture (non-UEIR): 3

Cruelty towards Life: 3

Cruelty towards God(s), Akua (M7): 3

Psychic Feedback (M7, Telepsi): 3

Occult Wars: 3

Social Assaults, Insults: 2, 3

DESTRUCTION:

Assault with Blades, Knives, Swords: 2, 3

Assault with Gunpowder-based guns: 3

Assault with Arrows, Thrown Weapons: 2

Assault with Explosives, Arson: 2, 3

Assault with other dangerous items: 2, 3

Hunting Accident: 1, 2

Vehicle Accident: 1, 2

General Destruction: 2, 3

Website Vandalism: 2

Graphics Distortion: 2

Computer Viruses: 3

Trojans, Hacking programs: 3

Cyber wars: 3

Cyber terrorism: 3

Hijacking Vehicles: 3

Car-jacking: 3

Disturbing the Peace: 1, 2

Inciting Violence, Profanity: 1, 2, 3

Causing Violence: 2, 3

Bullying: 3

Retaliation, Blackmail, Threats: 3

Revenge Destruction: 3

Other Destruction: 2, 3

TRAFFIC VIOLATIONS:

General Traffic Violations: 2, 3

Speeding, recklessness: 2

Following, Cutting in a lane: 2

Not Obeying Traffic Laws: 2, 3

Road Rage: 2, 3

DUI (Drunk Driving): 2, 3

Texting or using Internet while driving: 3

Other Distractions: 2

Ramming, slamming car: 2

Use of car horn to make noise: 2

Noisy Car alarms: 2

Evading Cars, or Police: 2, 3

Swerving in traffic: 2

Causing Accidents: 3

Not signaling while turning abruptly: 2

Not paying Fines, Citations: 2, 3

Creating Gestures while driving: 2

Distracting other drivers: 2, 3

Seeking to violate the Law (for fun): 3

Not Yielding to traffic: 3

Not respecting Right of Way: 3

Other Traffic Violations: 2, 3

SEX CRIMES:

Rape, induced: 3

Rape, non-consent: 3

Rape, pillage (town): 3

Rape, Gang: 3

Rape, with Permission: 2

Harassment: 2

Sexual Assault: 2, 3

Sex Drugs (Chloroform): 2, 3

Date Rape Drug: 3

Date Rape: 2

With Minor (age. 0-12): 3

With Disabled: 2, 3

With Elderly: 2, 3

With animals: 2, 3

Harassment, multiple: 3

Unwanted Advances: 2, 3

Incest (non-UEIR): 3

Cloning (non-UEIR) 2, 3

Polygamy: 2, 3

Promoting Gender bias: 2

Promoting Bisexuality, etc.: 2

Corrupting the Youth: 2

DEFIANCE:

Overuse of Force (Police): 2, 3
Lying to the UEIR about losing false wars: 3
Failure to adhere to UEIR Laws: 3
Seeking to violate this Law Code: 3
Seeking to Attack the UEIR: 3
Disobeying a command: 3
Perjury in UEIR Courts: 3
Disruption of Society, Insurrection: 3
Causing Corruption, Treason: 3
Causing Dissent among the people: 3
Trying to Overthrow UEIR: 3, 4
Trying to injure or kill UEIR Officers: 3, 4
Anti-UEIR Advertising: 3
Anti-UEIR Anything: 3
Spreading Lies about the UEIR: 2, 3
Spreading Lies about UEIR Officers (S7): 3
Deception of Taxes: 3
Deception in Tax collecting: 2, 3
Overall Defiance: 3
Causing Mischief: 2, 3
Causing Mayhem or Chaos: 3
Causing anti-UEIR propaganda: 3
Supporting Rogue Governments: 3

RELATIONSHIPS

Political Marriage (false union): 2

Marriage for Profit: 2, 3

Profit upon quick Divorce: 2, 3

Elder Marriages (deceptive intent): 2, 3

Ignoring Pre-Nuptial or Dowry: 2

Human + Animal Marriage: 2

Unofficial Marriage: 2, 3

Secular or State Marriage: 2

Hostile Divorce, Marriage: 2, 3

Hostile Take-over (Business): 3

Intimidation, threats (Civil): 2, 3

Hate Crimes, 3

Hate Crimes (Religious): 3

Hate Crimes (Ethnic): 3

Hate Crimes (Disabled): 3

Harassment, or by Media: 2, 3

Stalking, (& Celebrity): 2, 3

Undesired Union: 2, 3

Aggravation: 2, 3

Causing Fear: 2, 3

Causing Depression: 2, 3

Other Relations: 2, 3

Public Disturbance: 1, 2

LAWSUITS:

Unwarranted Lawsuits: 2, 3

Conspiracy Lawsuits: 3

Real Estate, Monetary Lawsuits: 3

Illegal Investigations: 2, 3

Invasion of Privacy: 2, 3

Obtaining Government Data: 3

Frivolous Lawsuits: 2, 3

Fame Lawsuits: 3

Waiving Right to Sue: 2, 3

Plebes Suing Citizens: 2, 3

Plebes Suing State: 2, 3

Immoral Class Actions: 2, 3

Waiving Moral Rights, TOS: 3

Property Lawsuits (owner): 2, 3

Trespassing, etc.: 2, 3

Simple Assault (Pushing) Suit: 2

Suits against Vizier or Pharaoh: 3

Suits against Consuls (M7): 3

Suits against Council of Elders: 3

Other Suits: 2, 3

False Indictments: 2, 3

Public Scandals (Media): 3

INTELLECTUAL PROPERTY:

Copyright Infringement (paid): 2, 3

Plagiarism (for profit): 2, 3

Obtaining Insignia: 2, 3

Obtaining Insignia (State): 3

Impersonation of Official: 3

Copyright (non-Fair Use): 2

Embezzlement (of Book, Music): 3

After the Fact (prior to Law): 2

Non-Body of Evidence: 2

Stolen Patent: 2, 3

Stolen Product: 2, 3

Website Vandalism, Excessive SPAM: 2, 3

Massive Use of Work (paid): 3

Massive Use of Work (unpaid): 2, 3

Poor Compensation (Civil): 2, 3

Not paying author of work: 3

Immoral Publication: 3

Other Infringement: 2, 3

Confidentiality Data Leakage: 3

Selling Trade Secrets: 3

PROPERTY LAWS:

Trespassing, Vandalism: 2, 3

Deliberate Injury on site: 2, 3

Accidental Injury on property: 1

Neglecting ownership (of Pharaoh): 2

Neglecting Land Lord Rights: 2

Neglecting Tenant's Rights: 2

Not yielding to Pedestrians, Other Life: 2

Not yielding to non-motor Vehicles: 2

Not Yielding to Children (in road): 1, 2

Flooding the Road with People: 2, 3

Riots on Public Land: 2, 3

Violent Protesters (Public): 2, 3

Immoral Confiscation: 2, 3

Causing Fires, Water Damage: 2, 3

Immoral Tax or Levy: 2, 3

Immoral Tax Audits: 2, 3

Failure to pay for Walls (repair): 2

Selling Stolen Property: 3

Seizing Stolen Property (non-UEIR): 3

Taxing Public Lands (beach): 1, 2

Other violations: 2, 3

AGRICULTURE:

Smuggling items in (snakes, etc.): 2, 3

Ruining Ecosystem: 2, 3

Smuggling via vehicle: 2, 3

Introducing Dangerous Crops: 2

Introducing Dangerous Life, insects: 2

Using Human Manure: 2

Unkempt Sanitation: 2

Causing Floods, Drought (non-Akua): 2

Importing Marijuana, (drugs): 2

Using Marijuana (non-medical), (Smoke): 2

Causing Pollution, smog: 2, 3

Causing Climate Change, smog: 3

Heaping Trash, Garbage: 2

Using Chemical Waste: 2

Not converting waste (recycle): 2

Not recycling usable materials: 2

Littering, Illegal Dumping: 2

Unlicensed Genetic Modification: 2

Not Protecting Rare Life Forms: 2

Polluting Beaches, waterways: 2

Other: 2, 3

RELIGIOUS LAWS:

Heresy, Blasphemy (against Divines): 2

Blotting out sacred images, Tikis: 3

Covering Statue Faces with Wax: 2, 3

Destroying Tikis or Idols: 2, 3

Pollution in or near Temples: 2

Attacks on Priesthood, Akua: 3

Imposing "Sharia Laws" on Niihau: 2, 3

Religious Terrorism, Destruction: 3

Stealing Temple Offerings: 2

Insulting Priests, Akua: 2

Desecrating Churches, Temples: 2

Burying Sinners on Holy Ground: 2

Burning "Marijuana Incense": 2

Veiled Threats (to Akua): 2, 3

Destroying Reading Materials: 2

Destroying Ritual Books: 2

Hate Crimes: 3

Inappropriate Use of Royal Seal: 2

Praying against the Akua: 2, 3

Willing people to death (Non-M7): 3

Touching Body of Akua: 3, 4

Spilling Liquid Offerings: 2

Other: 2, 3

KAPU (OTHER LAWS):

"Satanic Rituals" of Animal Sacrifices: 2, 3
"Voo-Doo" Astral Assault: 3
Unethical Business Practices: 2
Unethical Financial Services: 2
Denying anyone a Funeral Service: 2
Not cleaning up after a pet (Public): 1, 2
Sabotage, Website-Hostage: 3
Denying Fishing Rights to Natives: 2
Denying Natives their Rights: 2
Self-Employment Taxes: 2
Denying Citizen Lawsuit Rights: 2, 3
Denying Civil Rights: 2
Not Respecting International Law: 1, 2
Not Respecting UEIR Laws: 2
Seceding from State: 1, 2
Disallowing Pharaoh to Edit Laws: 2
Disallowing Vizier to Edit Laws: 2
Disallowing Alii to Edit Laws: 2
Failure to Crown Pharaoh: 1, 2
Failure to Protect Pharaoh or Alii: 2
Allowing USA to elect Pharaoh: 2
Allowing USA to interfere in politics: 2
Other: 2, 3

Citizen Civil Rights:

Citizens are registered in Duat or by a Duatian Officer (M7, S7), **not** on *Project Telepsi*. Each Citizen is protected by their Akhu, and can own property, marry or be single, worship their Gods if applicable, join peaceful groups, elect candidates for offices in the Republic, vote, obtain a home in Duat for their Afterlife, uphold the Principals of Ma'at in Society, spend money freely, obey UEIR Laws, etc.

Citizens are protected via *Diplomatic Immunity* in foreign lands, as the **UEIR has Sovereign Immunity** as well to prevent legal actions of foreign States or Nations. Each Citizen has a ***Secret Name*** given to them alone; this may be a name from their previous life via the UEIR in Duat. This is **similar to** a *Social Security number* in USA. **Only Citizens have Secret Names**, and this cannot be forged for the soul resonates with the word.

Plebes are non-Citizens and have limited rights. **Illegal immigrants** after staying one Calendar month in the Province should be registered or refrain from entering UEIR Property or buildings, unless they incur a Fee of $100 USD per day, **or until vacated**. Plebes related to Citizens are called **Knighted Citizens**, and have similar rights as Full Citizens. They just **cannot vote** for UEIR Candidates in the Republic.

Provincial Budget:

The UEIR Provincial Budget is established the First Month of each season. Each category is subdivided according to available funds. **The starting point is 100% or "One Million Dollars USD$" and is deducted by each subject from that amount.** If the revenue is less than that number, deduct as needed; if more, add as needed. **Viziers** (PM) Collects and Sets Taxes though Pharaoh has last word on purchases or expenditures.

Education, Temples, Technology: 10%

Military/Police/Firemen, etc.: 15%

Health, Social Services, etc.: 20%

Infrastructure, Roads, Housing: 5%

Farming, Food, Energy, etc.: 10%

Sanitation, Water, etc.: 5%

Servants, Insignia, Employees: 5%

Monuments, Museums, Tourism, etc. 5%

Welfare, Savings, Trade, Textiles: 20%

Other: 5%

Maat Freedoms:

1. **Freedom of Worship.** Citizens are allowed to worship any Egyptian Divine or its compatible equivalent; but not any religion that spawns undesirable behavior, riots, violence or protests, destruction, or fear.
2. **Presses and the Media** must report only Facts and recent information as made known to them by reporters. Other Media must declare its contents if Fictional on front and back covers (of any printed material), to prevent misinformation or delusions of its readers.
3. **Freedom of correct speech.** If spoken or recorded as Incorrect speech, it is the fault of the Citizen not the Government.
4. **Equal Rights of all Full Citizens.** Non-Citizens or visitors do not apply here. All Full Citizens have equal rights as specified.
5. **Fair Taxation and Non-Oppressive Taxes or non-confusing tax codes.**
6. **Economy: 2-Currency System.** A Popular Currency (maintained by Citizens) and a National Currency (for Government and Taxes).

7. **Citizenship Awards:** include tax exemption for 1 year.

Other Laws:

8. **Employment: Quality over Quantity.** Quality work will determine advancement not amount of products created.
9. **Teach Self-Control, Self-Restraint** of Citizens.
10. **Learn by Experience**.
11. **Don't gossip** about people in public if said people are suffering from any **paranoia disorders**, as this increases that effect.
12. **Legislation must be written with Wisdom** not on a whim (personal vendetta against society).
13. **Non-violent Crimes** will have the person experience a Deprogramming Session (using drugs & images or computer animation related to the crime) in a Mental Facility, until adapted. Then released after 1 week.
14. **Violent Crimes** will have a month of Deprogramming and be branded with an invisible Bar Code Tattoo or microchip. They will have limited Civil Rights and be given "medication for a fake illness" then released after

2 weeks of observation. They may also be used in forced labor.

Economy:

National Currency:

The *National Currency* is the **Kahelelani,** or "Island Shell," and is valued (paper currency) at the **set value** of a one-inch strand of that shell. Paper money may be printed as custom business cards, post cards, or as credit cards with **microchips** embedded in them.

Popular Currency:

The *Popular Currency* is valued in **Time Credits**, and will have a **hidden bar code** in invisible ink for tracking purposes (in case of theft, destruction, or misplacement). The paper version (etc.) will be a physical representation of the account of its bearer. Each Citizen will have a Bank Account of Time Credits, or "**Time Bank**." The account records transactions of goods or services, and each currency will have a starting value of 1.5 Hours of Time / Labor per Bearer; so you can trade Time Credits via the Time Bank and print out the paper version for physical transactions and the bar code will record this. PCs are each valued in $100 units of National Currency.

First set up an account at the Time Bank (*this was inspired by one Time Bank in San Francisco, CA in the early 2000s. It was a website with an accounting application that recorded units of Time in hours, each hour was valued at $10 USD. SF-BACE = San Francisco Bay Area Community Exchange*). **Then do things there** (barter exchanges, services paid by Time Credits, favors, gifts, etc.); these actions are recorded or deducted from the account. **Withdraw paper version printed** on a laser printer with bar code as an **interchangeable receipt**. Whatever you exchange outside of the system is recorded via the bar code. Popular Currency is decorated with **custom user artwork**, photos, or images. This may exist as a credit card type form, though some people prefer the feel of actual money. It may also be **printed with Braille** in paper form, as credit cards with this feature can become lodged inside a machine. Or whatever new technology the future prefers.

Popular Currency may be **traded** against National Currency in the way Gold Coins are traded at face value vs. gold content. A $20 USD Gold Coin at face value is still $20 USD; in terms of gold content this may be $1,000 USD.

PCs are worth either $100 NC or 1.5+ hour Time Credits of the Bearer to the Recipient.

Taxes & Revenue:

An offering to a Temple is like tossing coins into a water fountain – although it is **not mandatory, you do it anyway** for answering prayer or for good luck. Taxes are likewise not forced on the people. You pay taxes because you want to help someone, in this case the Government. Unlike charities that make people feel guilty about the neglected in asking for donations, Taxes are offerings from the heart, not the wallet. The Government's job is to **safeguard** the people, **not** steal from the poor **or cause hardship** because of low revenue income. If politicians can generate boatloads of money from a speech, they can also generate revenue from taxes in the same way. The Government can print its own revenue, but only needs some back for circulatory purposes. If people hoard money, this causes the Government to print more to **keep money in circulation.** Or if paper money is kept by a foreign nation or destroyed or misplaced, this is a problem. Collectors should buy only marked "Collector's items" not actual currency (inactive bar codes).

Offerings can be in other items other than currency.

Offerings should be about 1% to 10% **value of income** per month per Citizen's **profits**; no taxes collected if there are no profits per Citizen. Profits are from occupation of Citizen, **unless** it is a non-profit organization, welfare or disability, or retirement funds, etc. Companies may pay from 5% to 15% maximum. Anything over maximum will be sent to the Treasury for savings, or dispersed to Charity Organizations, Food Banks, Animal Services, Farms, Ranches, Medical Companies, or Education, etc.

Non-Citizens pay normal Tax Revenue **for every day** they are in the country, at 5% of Profits per Month of any non-classed income. This ends with either their return to their original or normal State or Country, or registration of Citizenship. Non-Citizens are **allowed up to one month** of Free Visitation Rights, per year.

Taxes are paid in National Currency or other offerings. Other offerings may include the following: wrapped or packaged Chocolate, tree nuts, salt, papyrus (Art), precious metals (gold, silver, copper, titanium, etc.), Health services (per hour), utility services (per hour), electricity (per day), bottled water, fresh bread or bread products, computers and components (flash drives, Tablet PC, printer paper...), etc.

Paper money in National Currency is **not limitless**. Popular Currency is limited by Time and life expectancy of the Citizens, or Labor. So abuse is limited. All Government officials **must account** for how much **is spent** per year, not be careless (like in USA, in causing debts from unforeseen income or non-income). NC cannot be devalued until the Shell it represents changes in value, which it won't. Therefore, the currency is permanently stable. The only **values** that change are in Foreign Currency (USD$, Yen, Pound, Euro, New Peso, etc.).

Should the Government not collect taxes, it will operate on a volunteer basis, or print money for its employees or use other currencies. Most likely it will use Popular Currency if otherwise. Should foreign nations have **military issues** and require the Pharaocracy to intervene (with our Magical Weapons) a **Tribute Tax** will be imposed on the nation requiring assistance and on the fallen foe at 15%+ of their spoils or net worth. We will **never intervene** "for free" if the actions **are costly**. The bird will have to flee its own cat; let Nature take its course.

Military:

The **Military** of the Pharaocracy may consist of actual soldiers (robots mostly), Psychic Warriors/Magicians, the Divines, or other specialists. All Citizens are encouraged to learn Martial Arts (self-defense mostly) in case of any disturbance. Placing **weapons** in the hands of normal Citizens is **discouraged** as it may contribute to unnecessary crimes or accidents.

If people **uphold the principals of Ma'at** then military intervention is unnecessary except to balance the social spheres, or contain *Isfet*. Sometimes people war over resources, social attacks, insults, women, or greed. But if people are consciously aware of their actions, **war becomes a fossil**.

Only people with Psychic potential should be educated in the military application of **Magical Effect**, or *Psychic Warfare* as it is called in the West. We wouldn't want children wizards getting killed now would we? Magical practices have an age starting limit at 23 years of age, with education at 17 years old. You **learn** about this from 17 on, as with the History and Practice of the effect. *Wiccans* are discouraged from applying before age 17.

As Magical Effect is both dangerous and lethal, age requirements are necessary. Prayer is a combination of telepathy (sending information) and **minor** Chronokinetic Energy Generation (CK-E). You *may become* Telepathic or Chronokinetic from practicing this, or via *Custom Genetics* (M7).

Genetic modification can create super soldiers capable of **Magical Effect**, once it is learned how this is possible (i.e. cloning M7). Until then you must be adapted from education and experimentation. Check out a local Occult Bookstore for your education, or a College Library. Practice Magic Spells, once a week until you are proficient in the spell, then move on to multiple spells per week and record results in a notebook. For a Spell in our culture, writing or speaking the Name of a Divine (sic) can cause an event. Ceremonies are physical spells with dramatic performances related to "movement." Military Magic uses chosen targets with environmental effects (earthquakes, storms, rain, etc.); and

protection enchantments are activated first in case of retaliation of the target or deflection. Writing your name in a circle or *Cartouche* is a protection rite, or *amulet*; in 2D (dimensional).

Martial Arts that are suggested are for mental and physical conditioning: Defensive & Offensive; Judo, Jujitsu, Karate, Tae Kwon Do, Kendo, Aikido, Tai Chi, Kung Fu, Archery, Fencing, etc. Once physical conditioning is learned, so the mental one can begin.

Officers:

Pharaoh (1), Vizier/Prime Minister (51), Alii (3), Council of Elders (10), Akua (up to 7), Chief Lector Priest (Kheri-Heb or Kahuna): (1), High Priest of the God AmonRa (1); Director of Ma'at (1), Chief of Police (2); Viceroy (Foreign Military: (1); Chief Economist (2), CEO of UEIR (M7, 1); Board of Directors (14); Treasurer (3), Secretary of State (2), Ambassador (2), Emissary (1), Technocrat (4), Chief Banker (2), Media (10), Imperial Guard (100), Bureaucracy (100), Health Director (4); etc.

Pharaoh's Duties:

Pharaoh is to promote and uphold the concept of Ma'at on Earth, and to oversee Legal Matters, Social Matters & Gatherings (religious or secular), attend ceremonies of State (awards, speeches, foreign events), oversee the enforcement of Law & Order, and spend taxes or buy items.

The **General Rule** is: whatever Pharaoh likes is permitted or Legal, and whatever Pharaoh dislikes is non-permitted or Illegal. Pharaoh as an instrument of Ma'at has **Sovereign Immunity**. Pharaoh is Chief Land owner (owns virtually everything) and can distribute taxes or other revenue to the State and to the People directly.

Every 30th year of Pharaoh's Reign is the event called a **Heb-Sed Festival**, whereby Pharaoh is tested, physically and or mentally, to determine fitness to continue ruling. If not, then another Pharaoh will be elected in his or her place. This may also occur every 15th year if necessary. The test can be anything from simple to moderate in complexity; a short run around a track, or a mental quiz or puzzle that the common Citizen can perform.

The **Council of Elders** is comprised of the eldest able adult (male or female) of each nuclear family. The Council decides on civil or criminal matters and can elect the Alii or Pharaoh via Secret Ballot. Vizier and other offices may be appointed by Pharaoh. The Council should consist of Residents from or on Niihau, and chosen representatives of Pharaoh or his associates, family, friends, or other Native Hawaiians or Portuguese members.

Native Rights are: allowing Natives from Niihau acreage or space for a home or residence, Free Fishing Rights, space for a Garden or Farm to grow food or fruit trees, right to be buried on Future Necropolis or be relocated there, right to wear traditional clothing, right to practice Native Culture without reprisal from State of Hawaii or Christian Missionaries, right to make cultural products (Niihau shell leis, flower leis, weapons or tools, etc.), right to an education in a school, college, or distance-learning class room; right to clean and purified water, and the right to own and care for pets.

The Alii will maintain these rights or add to them as needed. Future Pharaohs (or M7) may add or edit this Document to conform to the **Status Quo**.

Chapter 3: The Future of Ni'ihau Isle

In a matter of years, **Ni'ihau and all Pacific islands** *will be sunk by Climate Change and rising sea levels.* Who is going to tell this to the Natives? Are the Gods going to seize the island from Native Hawaii and swallow it in a new mythology, or will they allow M7 to help lift Ni'ihau into (post)-Modern times?

M7 already wrote volumes of this subject, on blogs and in books. **One book** found its way to the **Robinson family**, apparently. Besides wanting to help the islanders with his (*secret*) billions, **M7** wanted to develop his own Nation based there, *as a symbol of Ancient Egyptian Pharaohs* for the entire world to see. Perhaps build an Ancient Egyptian **walled city** or theme park, with statuary and reservoir-based waterfalls and tropical plants? Or use the **island as a Necropolis** (*the sand dunes hide Ancient Hawaiian burial sites anyway*), with Egyptian architecture – pyramids, temples, tombs, obelisks, sphinxes, Museums, etc.?

The Pharaocracy of America & Niihau: From Iniki to Empire.

by: Horus Michael

Copyright © 2014 HM-1

Genre: Political Science.

The Pharaocracy is a back-up Government should the USA Government shut itself down, however permanently. Some highlights are: focusing on Training rather than Technology for the Military (to reduce unwanted casualties in war), recruit soldiers after 2 years of Junior College (unmarried for less distraction), and allow Police/ Firemen/ Education/Technologies/Postal workers to be independent companies owned by the Pharaocracy of America & Niihau. Taxes will pay for the Pharaocracy, the remainder of which will repay the accumulated Debts of past Presidents and their corrupt administrations. Less emphasis on buying SOTA items will greatly reduce Government spending (SOTA = State of the Art). Taxes are a simple 10% Tithe of the population - no sales taxes or other taxes. Currency is the finite Kahelelani (Kah.), valued at: 1 Kah. = $1000 USD. National Anthem is the Conch Shell (1.5 minute exhale), National Animal is the Blue Whale or Monk Seal, National Religion is Pharaohism, Legal Codes are the Code Maat (Code Caesar Series), National Flower is the White Lotus, National Beverage is the Arnold

Palmer, and State Motto is "When Science fails, Fantasy prevails." Alternatives to Prison are: Public Humiliation (wear a sign with crimes on it in public), Subliminal Television with Psychedelic drugs, College Fraternity Hazing, Peace Corps or island exile, flogging with a leather whip, or other lesser forms. Military conscription (Psychic Warfare) starts when the candidate is proven to have an ability worth exploiting, and doesn't have to leave the country to use it. Freedom is accompanied by the willful responsibility of each citizen; the Military is not required to defend citizens who violate the freedoms of other countries by insulting foreign nations or their people, religion, culture, or beliefs. The Pharaocracy is governed by the Pharaoh and the Vizierate consisting of 1 Vizier per State; Consuls govern non-State Provinces. Each Vizier is a Law maker and enforcer. The Foreign Conquests of the Pharaocracy (classified top secret) influenced the condition of Climate Change by repetition of actions to influence the Elements (Weather manipulation via Psychic Wars).

About the Author:

Horus Michael follows the training of Ancient Egyptian Priests in his varied works on the Occult. He also studies Egyptian Archaeology. He currently lives in California, USA.

www.amazon.com/author/horusmichael

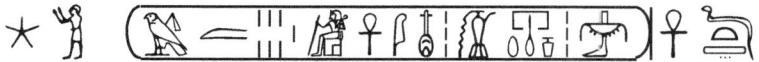

www.ingramcontent.com/pod-product-compliance
Lightning Source LLC
Chambersburg PA
CBHW060220290526
45789CB00003B/1348